SCHOOL LEADERSHIP AMIDST THE COVID-19 PANDEMIC

A Guide for Elementary School Heads Offering Modular Distance Learning

MAC DONALD P. JABONILLO

SCHOOL LEADERSHIP AMIDST THE COVID-19 PANDEMIC

A Guide for Elementary School Heads Offering Modular Distance Learning

ISBN 978-621-8307-05-6

Published by

Yawman Book Publishing House
Davao City Philippines
09219512458; yawmanresearch@gmail.com

Acknowledgments

I want to express my profound gratitude and wholehearted appreciation for the assistance, support, and encouragement of the following persons who made this work possible. I encountered many trials and challenges in writing this book, but my faith in God helped me develop the strength needed to complete this project.

I thank God for making me firm and steadfast; and blessing me with wisdom, good health, and tenacity to finish this endeavor.

Indeed, to God be the glory and honor;

To all School Heads of the Division of Panabo City who were part of this endeavor, thank you so much for your cooperation and for sharing your quality time, wisdom, and

To my wife, Jerly Mae Joy E. Jabonillo, and my daughter Majesca E. Jabonillo, who spent countless hours cheering me up to complete this task, "I appreciate your love so much".

Through the ebbs and flows of this book, I am forever grateful for your unconditional love and support.

Table of Contents

CHAPTER 1
LEADING IN TIMES OF CRISIS

School heads are leaders trusted by the local community to oversee and prepare educational programs designed to enhance student achievement and teachers' skills. Ancheta and Ancheta (2020) mention that public and private education institutions in the country and the world were severely afflicted by the COVID-19 pandemic, which began in December 2019. At the height of the pandemic, educational institutions came out with distance learning as an alternative solution. As a call of public demands and Deped mantra "No Children left, Behind," school leaders need to improve leadership practices.

In Pakistan, school heads suffered stress in reproduction, distribution, and transporting the self-learning materials (SLM's). Modules were often poorly written, and texts were challenging to digest by learners with disabilities such as dyslexia and the visually impaired (Burns, 2011). Likewise, Indira Gandhi National Open University (IGNOU) encountered problems reproducing, delivering, and retrieving learning materials in India. They found out that words used in their learning materials were beyond the level of the learners, and simplification of words must be done to understand (Dikshit et al., 2013) easily. In Malaysia, school heads received feedback from parents and guardians that Self Learning Modules (SLM's) or the printed modules did not cater to the students' different learning styles and needs (Cheng and Abu Bakar, 2017).

Problems with the Modular Distance Learning

In the Philippines, modular distance learning modalities have two major problems. The first is content; some have many errors that were far more serious than just typing or editing mistakes. DepEd also acknowledged that not all distance learning self modules or SLMs released this year had undergone "quality assurance" screening and promised to evaluate the material more rigorously in the future. Second, the expenses of the reproduction and distribution of printed modules had exhausted the funds available to schools (Manahan, 2020).

In the Division of Panabo City, it was observed that school heads have difficulty in managing the reproduction, distribution, and retrieval of self-learning materials (SLM's). Even if they received the monthly budget allocation of School Maintenance and Other Operating Expenses (MOOE), it was not enough and almost depleted. Other schools also received complaints like the delay of distribution, an insufficient number of copies, and some backlogs of modules in the assigned pickup stations. Also, in answering and understanding the module's content, not all learners answered and made the best output as they could be. On the other hand, some parents who did not have the opportunity to go to school also found it challenging to teach, guide, and assist their children at home.

This book cites examples from scenarios in four Districts of Panabo City Division. Moreover, various tasks have been made with regards to the development, effectiveness, and acceptability of modules for problem-solving and critical thinking skills of Alternative Learning System (Vergara, 2017), but none on the practices of school heads in the implementation of modular distance learning in new normal, especially in the Panabo City Division. This book provides additional information, ideas, strategies, and practices for school heads facing modular distance learning trends and challenges. It also has significance to society. For example, it raises the awareness and understanding of the value of (MDL) and helps discover several ways to learn amidst the odds and challenges to improve themselves.

The book is hinged on the Administrative Theory of Fayol (1916), who argued that organizational leadership should emphasize the management's human and behavioral factors. The Administrative Theory is based on the concept of departmentalization, which suggests that various activities to be carried out to achieve the organizations' common purpose should be categorized and classified into different groups or units such that the tasks can be accomplished effectively. The theory included fourteen management principles: delegation of labor, authority, duty, discipline, unity of command, unity of purpose, the subordination of individual interest, remuneration, degree of centralization, scalar chain, order, stable personnel, initiative, and spirit of the body. They were developed through observations and analyzed events that managers met in practice.

CHAPTER 2
MODULAR DISTANCE LEARNING

In the Philippines, the modular distance learning modality is the most popular learning modality currently used by all public schools. It is also a consideration of the learners in rural areas where the internet is not accessible for online learning. Based on the survey conducted by the Department of Education (DepEd), learning through printed and digital modules emerged as the most preferred distance learning method for parents with children who are enrolled this academic year (Bernardo, 2020).

In addition, Dangle and Sumaoang (2020) expressed that education is no longer held within the school due to the continuous onslaught of the COVID 19 virus. Parents served as partners of teachers in the delivery of instruction. Parents played a vital role as home facilitators. They were the ones to retrieve and submit the Self-Learning Modules (SLM's) from the schools or barangay halls or designated areas at the beginning and end of the week, depending on the agreement between the parents and the school. Further, they must check their child's schedule or workweek plan due to the numerous subjects or activities to be done and ensure to follow accordingly.

Moreover, Nardo M. B. (2017) reiterated that modules encouraged the learner's independent study. One of the benefits of using modules for instruction is acquiring better learning skills among students. It promotes a sense of obligation in fulfilling the duties provided in the module. With little or no support from others, the students improve independently. They learn by themselves; they are empowered.

Further, the teacher monitors the learners' progress in the modular distance learning modality (MDL). For example, students may ask for assistance from the teacher via e-mail, telephone, text message/instant messaging, among others. Also, where possible, the teacher shall do home visits to learners needing remediation or assistance (Llego, 2020).

Furthermore, Finol (2020) elucidated that modular distance learning (MDL) is an example of asynchronous learning or independent learning, where students learn depending on their own time and pace. Learners were also provided with self-learning modules (SLM's), workbooks, worksheets, and textbooks to support their self-learning process. Further, MDL had more variety and flexibility for teachers and staff; and increased adaptability of instructional materials.

Also, Dejene (2019) expressed that teachers in a large class suffered from fewer students' participation and a short time to answer, which may hinder the implementation of modular distance learning. And it is common to find students copying from other students of the same class or different classes regarding individual assignments in modular distance learning.

Moreover, Boholano and Jamon (2021) cited that teachers had also encountered obstacles in modular distance learning. They had to balance their time for printing and to sort the modules, marking the modules, doing the modules, and weekly home learning plans. In addition, they were complying with all the documents required to be submitted and to be accomplished as attachments for their Result-Based Performance Management System (RPMS). In addition, Li and Yang (2013) found that printed self-learning modules performed lower than those who used computers for animation learning modules compared with technology.

Furthermore, Dangle and Sumaoang (2020) asserted that in modular distance learning, MDL erroneous self-learning modules (SLM's) were released by DepEd in the field. Teachers and school administrators were given the task to double-check before delivering these to the learners. Thus, teachers in the area were tasked to make self-learning modules for the students. Also, DepEd Memorandum (OUA MEMO 00-1020-0138, 2020), known as DepEd Error Watch, aimed to intensify monitoring and evaluating the content of released self-learning modules (SLM's) by the Department of

Education. It also encouraged anybody to report errors found in different learning materials in Self Learning Modules, DepEd TV, DepEd Commons, and DepEd TV YouTube Channel.

In addition, Adonis (2020) cited, based on her report on Philippine Daily Inquirer, that there were 41 erroneous self-learning modules (SLM's) found by the DepEd's Error Watch and confirmed by Diosdado San Antonio, Education Undersecretary for curriculum and instruction, during a press conference. He also encouraged school heads and teachers to intensify the monitoring and checking of the self-learning modules before giving them to the learners.

Furthermore, Yoseph and Mekwanent (2015) expressed that lessons divided the assignment into small separated units in modular learning. It was independent, non-continuous, and mostly done in a short duration where learners collected credits of modules, resulting in the qualification required for such various credits. Students controlled their learning style and pace, which developed more learning responsibility. It also required more maturity on the learner's part. The self-learning modules were suitable for mature students.

Also, Hernandez (2012) emphasized that teachers needed to use feedback in a modular scheme, regularly monitor students' learning progress, and provide immediate and consistent feedback. They also stressed that the concept of assessing modular programs included evaluating the required skills, identifying difficulties, and demonstrating proficiency. The individual differences of the learners must be considered in providing flexibility in terms of pace, format, and teaching topics.

To address the gap and challenges encountered in implementing modular distance learning, DepEd Order (No. 32 s. 2020) was promulgated to ensure unhampered delivery of quality education service to its learners and community. The Department of Education hired a Learners Support Aid (LSA) to assist in reproducing self-learning modules, activity sheets, and other instructional materials. Their task was to monitor and track learners' accomplishments in the Weekly Home Learning Plan following the timeframe set by the teachers.

Olamo, et al. (2019) cited, based on their research study, that modular learning curriculum had not been favorably realized due to some difficulties in the implementation, like the unavailability of resources, supply of facilities and materials, the struggle of the reproduction of modules, and less participation of the learners. In addition, they reiterated that to have the adequate implementation of the said programs, the necessary materials, supplies, and facilities must be given priority to create a favorable condition for educators, learners, and school leaders.

Also, Casilao (2020) reiterated, based on her report on GMA News, that educators must suffer most because of the cumbersome tasks needed to accomplish in the Modular Distance Learning modality. There was a need to reproduce and check the self-learning modules (SLM's). Teachers were also urged to produce these modules despite tight resources, prompting them to resort to family and friends for assistance.

Furthermore, Sundarasen et al. (2020) in Malaysia cited that most students complained about modular learning due to the overwhelming number of self-learning modules, unclear and confusing content, and instructions that hinder students' learning development. Furthermore, the sufferings experienced by learners had a significant bearing on the stress and anxiety levels of the students.

Chapter 3
Roles of the School Heads

The school heads are responsible for the school's effective general management for ensuring the provision of academic leadership and strategic vision and for the quality of the student experience. In addition, they served as managers and mentors who empowered students and teachers in learning communities. In these new challenges brought by COVID-19, they needed to introduce new innovative modes of learning to continue education and achieve higher learning outcomes without compromising the welfare and safety of our learners (Republic Act (No. 9155).

In addition, Dangle and Sumaoang (2020) expressed that the disadvantages of modular distance learning (MDL) included greater self-discipline and self-motivation required for students. Increased preparation time, lack of concrete rewards for teachers and staff, and more significant administrative function to find and prepare additional resources needed to operate multiple modules. Bautista (2015) cited that the role of school heads implementing the modular distance necessary learning to be instructional leaders seem empowered, creative, transformational, valuable, driven, and not dependent on prescription. On the other hand, as chief executive officer, the principal was responsible for the smooth and efficient running of the school's finances, personnel, delivery of quality education, integrating and aligning curriculum, ensuring curriculum efficiency, and regularly evaluating and enriching updating the curriculum.

Carrying out the School's Vision And Mission

School heads were the essential leaders in the educational system in administering modular learning. They were responsible for carrying out the school's vision and mission. They played a vital role in schools' proper functioning, which affected all aspects of school operations. School administrators were responsible for instructional supervision and implementing all educational programs and projects. In addition, they had an essential role in achieving the government's goal of providing high-quality primary education (Muring, 2014).

Furthermore, school heads cover many different roles and responsibilities in school in modular learning. It included the leadership and management style of innovative ways to strengthen the new learning modality. They were also tasked to evaluate teachers regarding the teaching and learning process and student discipline. Becoming a practical school head is hard work and is also time-consuming. He/She must be balanced within all of his/her roles and work hard to make sure s/he does best for all active constituents. Finally, the school principal must become skillful in setting priorities, scheduling, and organizing task (Meador, 2019).

Also, Kelly (2020) cited that school heads in the new normal implementing the new learning modality such as; modular learning and blended learning needed to strengthen the collaboration within stakeholders, teachers, and staff to think out of the box and create innovative ways to handle school. School heads also encouraged other people to realize their goals in mind, to apprehend and work relentlessly with others.

Roles of School Heads in Learning Modality

Thakral (2015) reiterated that school heads had two roles or major functions in any learning modality, distance learning, modular learning, or blended learning. First is instructional supervision, where school leaders need to supervise teachers' lessons and guide them on enhancing the teaching and learning process, evaluating students' learning outcomes, and examining programs and projects. Their responsibility is to manage the school facilities and resources for administrative functions.

Problem-solving

Also, Kelly (2020) cited that school heads in this new normal education needed to have high problem-solving skills to reassess and provide concrete steps to solve school issues and concerns. School heads must also empower leaders by sharing their vision, good attitude, and fairness to their subordinates. Further, they must deal with sensitive issues, including student and staff health issues, difficult home conditions for students, teacher evaluations, disciplinary issues with staff.

Quality Improvement

Also, being a school head needs to be an instructional leader. Their role must be to improve the quality of education. Instructional leadership had been empirically identified in managing educational changes. It showed that it is still relevant to practice instructional leadership to address changes in education in the 21st-century; school administrators who act as instructional leaders must strive to be high-impact leaders to effectively guide the implementation of education system improvement (Aziz et al., 2017).

Evaluate School Programs

Likewise, a school head must evaluate and update school programs if appropriate every year. For example, if a reading program was stagnant and students did not progress, a school head should assess the program and make adjustments when necessary to develop it. The school head aspect can benefit from having good relationships with parents and other community stakeholders. Schools can significantly benefit from building relationships with local individuals and businesses. Benefits included in-kind donations, personal time, and school program support (Meador, 2019).

Besides, Boogaard (2020) expressed that an excellent school head didn't depend on their skills. They also need to ask for help from teachers and staff by having collaborative planning. They must have self-awareness and confidence to know when to call for help, like when one had no idea what to do when they made a mistake and needed additional expertise or insights about implemented programs and projects.

Furthermore, Krasnoff (2015) cited that successful school heads affected several schools' results, including influence and five primary responsibilities. To develop a vision of academic success for all learners based on high expectations, create a hospitable climate for learning to achieve security, and promote leadership in others. For teachers and other adults to share the school vision, enhancing instruction allows students to learn to their best, manage people, information and promote change in school.

Communication

Moreover, a good school head should listen to all sides of the issue without jumping to conclusions and collecting as much evidence as possible. Their position in the discipline of students was close to that of a judge and a jury. The school principal decided whether the student was responsible for disciplinary misconduct and what sanctions needed to impose. An effective principal consistently documented discipline issues, making fair decisions, and educated parents as needed (Meador, 2019).

Inspire

Besides, Mahlangu (2014) reiterated that school heads in a modular education system were expected to inspire, motivate, and appeal to teachers through various skills and practices. That communicate their value to their schools; these include the environment of confidence and cooperation, mutual and controlled mission, risk-taking and, ongoing professional development. So, the evaluation and giving technical assistance to the teachers was one of the essential responsibilities of school heads. They sought to use their observations and assessment tools to help staff learn new skills upskills and develop innovative best practices based on research – to help teachers become the best teachers they can be (Kraft and Gilmour, 2016).

Moreover, school heads' roles and responsibilities have evolved continuously over the last century in response to the changing educational environment and social expectations (Spillane and Kenney, 2012). School heads in the 21st century are building managers, vision holders, inspirational leaders, and professional development providers. They molded their teaching staff and motivated students through these complementary roles (Leithwood and Louis, 2011).

Managing feedback

Further, Newell et al. (2018) cited that school heads were required to deliberately add highly effective constructive feedback to their teachers to support teachers' professional development as they learn and grow while maintaining a professional learning culture. Additionally, Meador (2019) expressed that another challenging task of school leaders was creating a school calendar year. It was very time-consuming to make things right and make everything proper. The school head may need to build several schedules, including a bell, a teacher's duty, a computer lab, and a library schedule. The school heads would review each of these schedules to ensure that no one had too heavy a load.

Furthermore, Cuban (2014) school heads were always hired to manage schools, use data for decision making, plan and schedule schoolwork, oversee the budget, and do many other management tasks. They were also tasked to assist teachers in meeting state academic standards aligning with the curriculum.

Lastly, Buckner (2020) elucidated that school heads were responsible for their schools' overall operation and accountable for teaching and learning in their school. In particular, it increased its duty to supervise education and improve teachers' training. Moreover, principals were also responsible for facilitating their school's interactions with parents and others in the school community. It allowed teachers' internal and external stakeholders to be more involved and recognize that what they do matters in school success. Further, it would help parents and guardians follow up and update the queries and predicament of the lessons in the modules.

CHAPTER 4
ROLES OF THE SCHOOL HEADS IN THE NEW NORMAL

School heads needed to upskill and reskill their professional learning in the new normal learning modality. They need to learn more about technology, online conferencing platforms, and other strategies to enable distance learning to address. Continuing to learn about technology is also essential for school leaders because most of the schools' reports and programs are technology (Gunderson, 2020).

Crafting Contingency Plans

In addition, Rice (2020) stated that school heads need to craft contingency plans that will produce a comprehensive policy that proactively addresses the challenges and difficulties of implementing new normal education in times of this crisis. Further, this Learning Continuity Plan (LCP) of school heads responds to the recent adversities of learning. All learning modalities, collaborating with the school community, and monitoring programs are indicated for the whole school year.

Monitor And Check The Programs, Projects, And Budget

Moreover, Paragoso and Barazon Jr (2019) cited that to monitor and check the programs, projects, and budget allocated in the new normal learning modality are appropriately utilized, the department of education mandates the school heads to intensify the School Monitoring and Evaluation Assessment and Adjustment (SMEA) to improve the delivery of Basic Educational Services. In addition, it included educational resources, which usually focus on liquidating the school Maintenance and Other Operating expenses (MOOE), liquidating the PTA funds, income-generating programs, providing local school board funds, and other funds donated by partners and other stakeholders.

Establish Strong Linkages with Stakeholders

Furthermore, Jager (2019) elucidated that school heads need to establish strong linkages with the stakeholders to successfully implement modular distance learning (MDL) in this new normal learning modality. By building good rapport relationships, one can create a favorable environment of support and trust and establish cooperation in school. As a result, schools can foresee possible hindrances and manage stakeholders' expectations more effectively to solidify their long-term success.

Supervise Teacher and Staff

McCarty (2020) also expressed that time is a challenge in the new normal education. School heads demanded that teachers and staff quickly do different things, like preparing self-learning modules and updating reports through the internet. It's a new challenge and, at the same time, an opportunity to learn not only for the students but also for the school heads and teachers, who need to adapt to the new normal education.

Moreover, Friday (2020) cited that school heads need to be flexible in the new normal situation because it is vital. They needed to be open-minded by having a rapport communication between teachers, students, and parents. Teachers also needed to be flexible and consistent to help minimize confusion for parents regarding the new learning mode. Further, the transitions to remote instruction helped remind school principals that their priority was always the students.

Monitor Compliance to Protocols

Furthermore, School heads also reiterated that another big problem of the new normal education is disrupting school routines, like following the social distance and adhering to safety protocols that students and adults had never experienced in this environment. They also strengthen the school premises that wearing face masks is necessary to enter the building, which poses a problem because no one wants to wear them, but it is needed for schools' safe operation (Anderson, 2020).

Likewise, Bender (2020) emphasized that the COVID 19 virus is still continuously ruining the educational sector in the new normal learning modality. As school leaders, they were given a significant task to combat this latest adversity. School heads must guarantee that they advocate disseminating information within their school community, including preventive and control measures and following the health authorities' guidelines.

Evaluation Of The School Improvement Plan

The continuous onslaught of the COVID-19 pandemic had heavily affected and caused difficulties to the education sector. Following this, school heads' were mandated to undergo meticulous investigation and evaluation of the school improvement plan (SIP) and modify respectively to respond to the conditions and eventualities in the school field. In addition, school heads should assess their "hierarchy of needs" and potential problems without jeopardizing the health and welfare of learners, teaching, and non-teaching personnel in the school (DepEd Order No. 15 s. 2020).

In addition, Vergeire (2020) cited that school heads in the new normal scheme play a significant role in protecting, preventing, and monitoring the school community against the COVID 19 pandemic. Therefore, there should be proper coordination with the local communities and local health authorities to track and quarantine confirmed cases and enough medical equipment such as PPE, alcohol, masks, and face shields in school premises.

Malipot (2020) stipulated that in new normal education, the primary private education and non-DepEd institution were authorized to continue their respective school openings as long as they provide distance learning. However, parents insisted that the 'homeschooling' scenario was unfavorable to the students due to the factors that could distract their attention, like watching television, computer games, and mobile devices typical at home. This statement, which was supported by Burgess and Sievertsen (2020), stipulated that homeschooling is a massive shock to parents and students' social life and learning.

Promoting Online Learning

Watson (2019) described that they offered different learning modalities like modular, online learning, and blended learning modalities in the new normal. Combining online and offline learning gave learners time to undertake various performance tasks at their own pace through teacher-student interaction and offline learning using a particular platform.

Education on Emergency Response Measures

In addition, Henebery (2020) reiterated that school heads were tasked to navigate their staff and students through the emergency response of the COVID-19 virus in new normal education. The need to upskill and reskill information technology skills by creating new opportunities to connect with people virtually was significant in this new normal. School heads needed to evaluate and structure the curriculum to make learning easy and understandable. Further, this recent adversity allows us to rethink and innovate on how we deliver programs, engage students and staff, and test new strategies to enhance learning.

Mentor Faculty and Staff

School heads needed to intensify their leadership capability to mentor their teachers, navigate this experience, and broaden their classroom resources, teaching strategies, and creative communication practices in this new normal. In addition, the school head must be a pollinator and innovative. In this scenario, school heads needed to learn to enhance access by assessing financial capacity, developing their digital foundation, and addressing this crisis's needs (Hall, 2020).

Promoting Professional Development

The continuous professional development (CPD) of school leaders and teachers is essential to develop professional and personal qualities as educators to enhance and hone their teaching skills and strategy. Further, teachers should reskill and upskill to cater to the learners' different needs and equip on the current education trends in the new normal education.

In the new normal education, many families suffered from financial crises due to losing jobs and the closure of enterprises affected by community quarantine. Therefore, school heads must create a school selection committee to screen and evaluate qualified students for the provision of subsidies and allowances from private and public elementary and secondary education (Republic Act, 11494).

Monitoring and Evaluation

Miller (2020) cited that school heads must intensify schools' monitoring and evaluation systems in the new normal education. They played an essential role in the school's accountability, growth, and development. It can only be realized through record-keeping and securing Means of Verification (MOVs) to understand and learn from the past to improve the programs and projects and allocate the resources properly.

The Sulong Edukalidad of the DepEd responded to the low quality of education here in the Philippines. It prioritized access to quality education and ensured that no Filipino learner was left behind. The approach of school heads in this 'new normal' must work with patriotism, compassion, and sensitivity. They ensured that education would not burden our parents, learners, and teachers but see a silver lining amidst these new predicaments. Despite the difficulties along the way, they guaranteed that they strike the balance of giving quality education and considering each other (The Department of Education, 2019).

Lastly, Dangle and Sumaoang (2020) cited that school heads in the new normal implementing modular distance learning should intensify home visitation once a week to identify the students' status and follow up on the learning updates of students. Further, the school may initiate a limited face-to-face class if the area is low at risk of the COVID-19 virus. And schools may add or venture other learning modalities to support modular distance learning (MDL).

Briones (2020) cited to continue education amidst the pandemic circumstances, school heads in the new normal needed to craft a school-based learning continuity plan (SBCLP). It is a concrete guide for every school head in implementing its new learning modality such as; blended learning, online learning, modular distance learning (MDL). In this order, teachers can still deliver instruction in a safe work and learning environment amidst the COVID-19 pandemic.

In addition, DepEd, Division Memorandum (No. 188, s. 2020) was issued to command all school heads at their designated schools to create a learning continuity plan (LCP) to continue providing access, quality, and liberating education under the new normal of basic education in the school year 2020-2021. It also aimed to ensure adherence to policies and guidelines set by DepEd, LGU, DOH, and IATF to protect the welfare and safety of our students, educators, and stakeholders.

Today, the COVID-19 virus is still destroying the country, and among those that were drastically affected is the education sector. In the new normal scenario, school heads played a vital role in following the proper safety protocols, monitoring the school personnel who manifested COVID-19, and extending the school campus' implementation and safety protocols (Ancheta and Ancheta, 2020).

Moreover, school heads are not about personality. It's about behavior, an observable set of skills and abilities. Kouzes and Posner (2012) cited The Five Practices of Exemplary Leadership; Model the way, Leaders establish principles concerning the way teachers and staff should be treated. They should pursue goals; Inspire a shared vision; imagine the future; think outside the box of what an organization can become. Create new ideas to change the process; they look for innovative ways to improve it. Enable Others to Act; leaders foster collaboration and build spirited teams. Encourage the Heart; accomplishing extraordinary things in organizations is hard work.

Furthermore, Tingley (2017) shared his best practices of being a school leader. School heads must be visible at school and visit classrooms as a part of their instructional supervision to monitor students' performance and teachers' concerns regarding the teaching-learning process. Further, work with their employees to find solutions communicate clearly and effectively. School heads also needed to keep teachers informed of what's going on, always respect and support teachers and staff, and not play favorites.

Wallace Foundation (2013) published the five practices to be an effective school administrator; 1. Be a vision holder for the academic success of all learners based on excellent standards. 2. Create an academically conducive environment for learners. 3. Cultivate others' leadership so that teachers and other adults can play their part in embodying the school's vision. Inspire teachers to continue their professional development to do their best to teach. Students can learn to the fullest, and lastly, manage people, data, and processes for school improvement.

Gura (2019) cited that school heads needed to embrace change in the new learning modality wholeheartedly to fight the continuous disruption of the COVID-19 virus, which brought us fear and extreme change in the educational sector. Instead, they consciously choose to keep moving onward and continue improving and growing as better school leaders by embracing and accepting change.

In addition, Heathfield (2020) cited that being positive is an essential practice that school heads need to address the new adversities in this new normal scenario. An optimistic outlook will positively impact one's health, comfort, and performance. Further, optimism is one factor that can affect school heads' success and self-fulfillment.

Positive Mindset

Reh (2020) cited that one of the best practices of a good school head in implementing modular distance learning is being positive-minded despite numerous difficulties implementing the new learning modality. It can boost and motivate the morale of their constituents to be more compassionate to realize the company's success. Having a positive outlook can also help them be more productive, efficient, and efficiently manage tasks.

Use of Activity Sheets and Instructional Material

Also, Melton (2014) expressed that one of the best practices of school heads in implementing modular learning was that schools provided activity sheets and instructional material to the learners. The students need to increase the positive output, enhancing their reading and writing capability. Teachers can assist in a crucial professional duty by providing learning materials differentiating instruction to the learners. Effiong and Igiri (2015) supported that school heads need to recognize that in giving different instructional materials. These learning materials could enhance students' learning performance that complemented teachers' effort in the teaching-learning process.

Open Communication

Vdovin (2017) cited that school heads should establish open communication at schools, such as school websites and group chats, in every classroom in implementing modular learning. The querries of the lessons, feedback, and suggestions will cater to the department's betterment. Further, it will lead everyone to be on the same page, moving in the same direction toward the same goal. Creating an open environment at school can lead to more remarkable job accomplishment, reduced stress, support, and mutual respect.

Interest in Employees

A well-rounded school leader is an essential component of leading effectively in a dynamic, evolving society. Versatile leaders have more interest in employees and persuasive teams. We are now in globalization, and it's necessary to cooperate with people with different backgrounds and ability levels effectively. It required a more flexible approach to problems and solutions (Schindler, 2020).

Showcase School Programs and Projects

Madsen (2020) cited that a school head needed to build strong linkages with the stakeholders in implementing modular distance learning. When you give time to understand and showcase your programs and projects at school, it can enhance dynamic communication and a strong relationship. They tend to be more open, compassionate, and motivated in what you may have to speak when you actively engage and appreciate their situation. They will also help you address the challenges and augment the modular learning modality.

Dynamism

There is nothing permanent in this world, and we will go through changes over time. It may be sensitive, spiritual, physical, or mental, and sometimes it may happen to us without a plan. Further, school heads need to adopt this new learning modality. Each change means a new learning opportunity to evolve and hone themselves as great leaders (Coaching, 2019).

Every person in the community is a stakeholder. They play an essential role in supporting the educational system. School heads should build and maintain rapport relationships with other stakeholders to augment the implementation of the modular scheme, as this will allow everybody to work together, which will positively impact the school harmoniously (Saxena, 2014). School heads should value the partnership of internal and external stakeholders and local government units (LGUs) to support quality education. "All school stakeholders, partners, and supporters are essential to improve public schools, donated buildings, and they have helped our teachers and learners whenever the need arises," as Education Secretary Leonor Briones stated (Montemayor, 2019).

Guarantee Quality Education

Abu (2020) cited that every Filipino's noble right is to access quality education despite the crisis our country and other nations are experiencing. School heads must guarantee that education must continue without compromising the health, security, and welfare of all students, teachers, and personnel at school. Yukl & Mahsud (2010) elucidated that one of the best characteristics of school heads is being a versatile and adaptive leaders in a world full of stress, challenges, difficulty, and changes. School leaders must maintain a high commitment to do necessary and ethical. Further, being a versatile leader must deal with problems and challenges in innovative ways and look at this as an opportunity to develop as a great leader.

Strenthen the Parents-Teachers Association

In addition, school heads should build a good partnership with the stakeholders that will augment the implementation of modular distance learning, as DepEd Order (No. 54, s. 2009) stated that school leaders need to establish a Parents-Teachers Association (PTA) for both elementary and secondary schools to administer a conference to exchange opinions, discuss issues, and formulate solutions associated with school programs. Finkelstein and Repeta (2017) emphasized that solid linkages of stakeholders must be given importance as it allows sharing ideas that will help the success of schools. A true value-add partnership is defined by the freedom to communicate, advocate, discuss, and have challenging discussions that drive innovative growth and improvement of schools.

Collaborate with School Community

Furthermore, Sharp (2019) cited that one of the practices of school leaders is being collaborative with teachers and stakeholders to have a smooth and successful implementation in the school. Seeking help is vital for everyone and the organization. It's a sign of strength and courage, reduces the expense and impact of weakness, and allows more people to grow, flourish, and contribute to a more positive community.

School leaders must recognize the cooperation of stakeholders as they help augment the modular distance learning modality at school. The participation of stakeholders is important because they have a good potential to produce positive change in schools, especially in this time of the pandemic. In addition, they offer donations such as giving equipment to reproduce self-learning modules (SLM's), contributing to information decimation regarding the modular scheme (kahootz.com, 2020).

The cited literature discussed and elaborated the concept of modular distance learning modalities and the school head's essential role in implementing learning modalities. The performance of the Modular Distance Learning modality is the responsibility and accountability of the school administrators. They need to employ effective and efficient strategies while considering that resiliency can contribute to implementing learning modalities. School leaders need to address problems they encounter along the way and improve their students' learning outcomes.

CHAPTER 6
LIVED EXPERIENCES AND PRACTICES OF ELEMENTARY SCHOOL HEADS

Table 1 shows elementary school heads' lived experiences and practices on modular distance learning in the new normal.

Table 1. Lived Experiences and Practices of the Elementary School Heads on in the New Normal

Major Themes	Core Ideas
Crafting the School-Based Learning Continuity Plan	• Using the learning continuity plan as the blueprint • Having crafted the learning continuity plan as the road map • Being required to formulate the school learning continuity plan • Crafting the school-based learning continuity plan with the teachers
Establishing Strong Linkages with the Stakeholders	• Seeking support from stakeholders • Establishing linkages with barangay, PTA and other stakeholders • Tapping possible stakeholders especially in financial matters • Having strong partnership with the private stakeholders • Being resourceful to tap other stakeholders for the provision of materials
Embracing Change	• Welcoming change instead of treating it as a problem • Accepting change in this difficult situation

	• We adjust and adopt the new modality of learning • adopting the new normal thru technical assistance to teachers • Having a new learning experience everyone is adjusting to the new modality • Opening one's heart to adopt the MDL
Finding Clerical Errors	• Receiving complaints from the parents on the clerical errors • Having noticed clerical errors in the module • Receiving complaints on the typographical errors of modules. • Having noticed some clerical errors in the modules
Struggling in the Reproduction of SLMs	• Having problem with the lack of printing equipment and materials in the market • Delaying the printing of the modules also delayed the delivery of learning • Having scarcity of printing materials challenged the school administration • Going home late just to finish printing the learning modules
Giving Supplementary Materials	• Giving of reading materials every week to enhance students' learning • Providing supplementary activity sheets to students • Giving MELCs-based activity sheets and reading materials

Crafting the School-Based Learning Continuity Plan

The survey responses pointed out that the school heads crafted a school-based continuity plan that served as a road map for the continuity of education amidst the pandemic.

Accordingly, IDI03 expressed:

> *"Sa School-Based Learning Continuity Plan (SBLCP) mao ang blueprint nga gayd nato for this school year 2020-2021."*

(School-Based Learning Continuity Plan is the blueprint that will serve as our guide for this school year 2020-2021)

Also, IDI04 had the same experience when he stated:

> *"Ginapahimo mi ug school-based continuity plan for the continuation of that modality and then gi-present namo sa among Schools Division Superintendent."*

(We crafted a school-based continuity plan to continue that modality and was presented to our School Division Superintendent.)

In the same way, IDI05 supported the claim saying:

> *"School heads are required to formulate Learning Continuity Plan that will serve as the road map for running the school year 2020-2021."*

(School heads were required to formulate Learning Continuity Plan that served as the road map for the school year 2020-2021)

Also, IDI06 expressed that,

"We had this School Based Continuity Plan (SBLCP), and we created this together with my colleagues and co-teachers."

(We had this School Based Continuity Plan (SBLCP), and we created this together with my colleagues and co-teachers.)

IDI08 relatively shared:

"Sa eksperyens murag daghan najud kaayo. From the very start nag buhat ug kanang Continuity plan, augmentation na strategy sa learner's para mapadayon ang learning sa mga bata sa school year."

(As to experience, it seemed like there's a lot. From the start, we made continuity plans for the continuity of education of our children.)

Contingency Plans

Crafting a school-based continuity plan was revealed as one of the contingency plans of each school amidst the pandemic, which served as a guide for the continuity of our children's learning.

The COVID-19 pandemic has created challenges in educational institutions that were not experienced before. In response to this new adversity, the Department of Education

(DepEd) mandated school heads to craft a School-based Learning Continuity Plan (SBLCP) to guide 2020-2021. Participants uttered that having a preparation does more than prepare you for what to expect; it puts you in a position to handle what you didn't see coming. Furthermore, the SBLCP is a contingency plan for every school head in implementing each school's activities and programs. It provided learning opportunities for all learners while securing the safety of students, teachers, and stakeholders during public health emergencies, natural disasters, or any other extraordinary circumstances that might arise.

This claim was supported by Rice (2020) stated that school leaders recognized the need to prepare to produce a comprehensive policy that proactively addresses the difficulties and limitations they may face throughout the implementation of their learning continuity plan in their respective schools and districts. Learning Continuity Plan (LCP) was also a response to the new adversities of learning, such as natural catastrophes, public health crises, or other unusual situations.

In addition, crafting the School-Based Learning Continuity Plan was confirmed by Briones (2020), who expressed that these were contingency plans that enabled learners to continue learning and for the teachers to deliver instruction in a safe work and learning environment amidst COVID-19 pandemics. Further, it covered essential education requirements, such as the Most Essential Learning Competencies (MELC) modality of learning and health standard in schools and the workplace.

Moreover, this was also supported by the DepEd, Division Memorandum (No. 188, s. 2020), which reiterated that Learning Continuity Plan is a comprehensive plan of the Department of Education to continue providing quality education despite COVID- 19 pandemics. With this, school heads needed to craft the LCP together with the teachers and staff to continue education and to preserve the welfare and security of our students, educators, and stakeholders.

CHAPTER 7

ESTABLISHING STRONG LINKAGES WITH THE STAKEHOLDERS

The survey unveiled a strong linkage with the stakeholders that enabled them to work harmoniously, positively impacting our students.

IDI01 narrated with conviction:

"Mao nga kaylangan jud nato ug partnership, support from our stakeholder's kay kung magsalig ra jud ta sa atoang MOOE, kulang jud siya that is why maningkamot ta to have stakeholders to get donations from them."

(We need partnership and support from our stakeholders for donations since our MOOE is not enough.)

Likewise, IDI03 expressed her involvement:

"Also, to establish strong linkages with barangay, PTA, parents, stakeholders, and support and cooperation so mao nani siya nabutang to diri ang house to house distribution and retrieval sa mga modules."

(We also established strong linkages with the barangay, PTA, parents, and stakeholders for their support and cooperation for the house-to-house distribution and retrieval of modules.)

Relatedly, IDI06 persuaded:

"Kaylangan makig collaborate ka with the stakeholders, you tap with the possible

stakeholders to the implementation of this modality kasi, financial speaking may challenge talaga."

(We also need to collaborate and tap possible stakeholders that will help us implement MDL, especially in financial matters.)

Likewise, IDI07 expressed her involvement:

"Pero, ang isa sa good eksperyenses sa mga modular scheme, lipay pud ko sa strong partnership with the private stake holders. Wala namo nabati nga nagkulang mi ug mateyals og supplies to supplement sa mga pagkukulang sa atoang department diba."

(I am happy with this modular scheme because we had a strong partnership with private individuals who gave us printing materials and supplies to supplement the need of our department.)

IDI09 supported the notion and said:

"As a school leader, you should be resourceful enough to tap other stakeholders in providing materials for the modules."

(As a school head, you should be resourceful to tap other stakeholders in providing materials for the modules.)

Stake Holders and Modular Distance Learning

After a thorough analysis of the transcription, it was revealed that establishing strong linkages with the stakeholders was essential for the augmentation of the modular distance learning modality.

Most participants stated that establishing strong linkages among stakeholders will build a strong foundation of partnerships that will help and support providing quality educational services to our learners. Implementing MDL in the new normal, stakeholders play an essential role in learning using this modality; thus, both school and stakeholders could work harmoniously.

In this connection, Jager (2019) agreed that establishing strong linkages with the stakeholders was an imperative component that defined the success of a leader. Maintaining good relationships laid a foundation for creating an environment of support and trust and establishing a cooperation network. As a result, the organization can anticipate potential problems and manage stakeholders' expectations more effectively. In addition, stakeholders played an essential role in modular distance learning by providing financial support, materials, and equipment to augment this new learning modality.

Also, Madsen (2020) supported his statement that the capacity to develop genuine and lasting connections with stakeholders was one of the key ingredients to becoming victorious leaders. When one gives time to understand stakeholders, it could enhance dynamic communication and a strong relationship. The stakeholders played a vital role in schools' delivery of modular distance learning. They were the partners of the school heads in making school conducive to the teaching and learning process.

CHAPTER 8
EMBRACING CHANGE

One of the major themes of the survey was embracing change. All participants shared their experiences and practices on modular distance learning in the new normal.

IDI02, shared with a smile:

"Nalipay man gud ko in some part nga na challenge pud mi mga school heads sa Modular Distance Learning, makita nako nga hala! unsa kahay kanang bag-o karon, para kaning learning moabot jud sa bata instead na nagiging problem siya sa akoa."

(I am happy at the same time we were challenged about Modular Distance Learning, on what's new for our students to learn instead of thinking it as a problem.)

On the other hand, IDI03 aired out:

"To embrace the change, do something beautiful those something different, do something kanang amazing bitaw out of this difficult situation."

(To embrace the changes in this new modality, we have to do something different and amazing by seeing its positive side despite this difficult situation.)

Relatedly, IDI04 sensibly shared:

"For me as a school head nag adjust ako doon sa 1st month, pero naka adopt na kami. Wala na tayong magagawa kasi ito na talaga ang new

normal, whether we like it or not this is our new normal modality."*

(As a school head, I tried to adjust during the first month, but later on, I adopted it; we had no choice because whether we like it or not, this is now our new normal learning modality.)

Also, IDIo5 had the same experience when he stated:

"Automatically, we embrace and adapt what do we call this new normal. We provide all the necessary materials, necessary technical assistance to our teachers and including our learners."

(We embraced the new normal and provided necessary materials and technical assistance to our teachers and learners.)

IDIo6 uttered that:

"This modular distance learning is very new to all of us, murag karon pajud nato ni naeksperyens because of the pandemic, murag tanan jud ta nag adjust sa bag-o nga modality."

(Modular Distance Learning is very new to all of us. This is our first time to experience this kind of learning scenario brought about by this pandemic, and everybody was trying to adjust this modality.)

IDIo7, shared with a smile:

"We are kanang open heart to adopt Modular Distance Learning because we have one system, we have one department so dili man pwede nga imuhang gusto maoy matuman."

(We wholeheartedly adopted this Modular Distance Learning because we had one system and one department, that is why we cannot push or pursue things we wanted to implement.)

Embracing Change in Education

Hence, adapting to change is imperative to survive, grow, and succeed in modular distance learning.

The Philippines and the world's learning modality had drastically changed brought about by the COVID-19 pandemic. Most participants uttered that they needed to embrace changes wholeheartedly and do something beautiful despite this difficult situation. In this new normal environment, school heads implementing modular distance learning (MDL) promptly provided all the necessary materials technical assistance to our teachers and our learners to continue learning without jeopardizing the health and welfare of teachers and parents. Living the routinary tasks and comfort zone was not easy. Still, changes must be accepted for the service of the Filipino learners and responding to the call of duty of the department. Embracing change gave the school heads opportunities to learn and grow. Further, it can explore new things and opportunities to contribute to good leadership. And lastly, embracing changes can bring success, triumph, and victory if taken positively.

Gura (2019) stated that embracing change is essential, and it exists. It will help us improve our perspective and approach to living a more comfortable and more fulfilled life. We consciously choose to keep moving onward and continue improving and growing into better people by embracing and accepting change. In these challenging times brought about by the COVID-19 pandemic, school heads needed to embrace changes wholeheartedly to perform his/her duty being school leaders. The beauty of change is that it brings new possibilities.

Moreover, Coaching (2019) supported that we would change over time. It may be emotional, spiritual, physical, or mental, and sometimes it may happen to us without a plan. With each change, we can integrate new information into our character and sense of personhood. Change is a vital and potent part of life and an opportunity to grow.

Chapter 9
Finding Clerical Errors

The survey showed that school heads receive feedback from parents most of the time regarding the blunders or errors of self-learning modules.

IDI01, with a deep breath, shared:

"Naay mga feedbacks sa mga ginikanan specialy sa first quarter sa implementation, there are complain sa error content sa atong module."

(In the first quarter of implementation, we received feedback from our parents regarding some errors in the content of the modules.)

Further, IDI02 expressed his sentiments, especially on the erroneous modules he narrated:

"Unta lang before jud erelease ang module kinahanglan sa ug thorough nga proof reading. Kasi ang nangyari man gud kung atong mapansin daghan jud kayo ug report nga daghan ug clerical error ang module."

(I hope that before releasing modules, there should be thorough proofreading, as we observed, there were a lot of complaints from our recipients regarding the clerical error in the modules.)

IDI07 unveiled similar feelings with displeasure, she said:

"Daghan tag mga eksperyenses on the modular system. At first daghan jud siyag reklamo specially the description, typographical error of the module."

(We had a lot of experiences in modular learning, we received complaints regarding the description and typographical errors of modules.)

Complaints had been heard coming from the parents due to the clerical errors in the modules as stated by IDI010:

"We notice that some clerical error in the modules, some parents chat, sending messages that ma'am, the answer to this is wrong, so we explain to the parents that it is a typo clerical error."

(We noticed some clerical errors in the modules; some parents chatted, sent messages, and complained about wrong answers to some questions. So, we explained to the parents that these were typoclerical errors.)

Modular learning is an important vehicle in transmitting learning while securing students' safety on the threat of COVID-19 viruses, specifically in areas where internet access is unavailable. The module's content must contain facts, and information read from the learning materials must be accurate and correct as this could affect students' learning outcomes. Most participants were bothered by the erroneous content of modules they encountered in implementing modular distance learning. They asserted that the consequences of committing faulty self-learning modules (SLM's) could be devastating. It would mean incorrect knowledge acquired by the students. And to address these challenges, school heads and teachers must thoroughly check the SLM's before giving them to the learners. This could also affect the pace of printing and preparation of modules.

In line with this, Dangle and Sumaoang (2020) proved that there were errors found in the content of the modules and that revisions of modules with mistakes were done in the field. Further, there were no modules from the central office, especially in MAPEH and Journalism-Filipino. Thus, teachers in the field were tasked to make the self-learning modules for the students.

In accordance with this, Adonis (2020) elucidated that self-learning module were found to have errors by the Department of Education (DepEd). It was recently confirmed through statements of Diosdado San Antonio, Education Undersecretary for curriculum and instruction, press conference. He explained that erroneous modules were in Math 2 modules. Another module in Davao Region categorized "red" as a shape instead of color. The erroneous and unclear instructions found in the self-learning modules were commonly found in social media. Thus, the department made initiatives to solve this problem by having a DepEd's Error Watch.

In response to numerous reports about the errors found in the self-learning modules released by the Department of Education, the office of The Undersecretary for Administration (OUA) announced the DepEd Error Watch initiatives. This was to receive and collate reports of errors found in the Self Learning Modules, DepEd TV, DepEd Commons, and DepEd TV YouTube Channel. Through these initiatives, anybody could improve the learning modality, specifically the MDL (DepEd Memorandum OUA MEMO 00-1020-0138, 2020).

CHAPTER 10

STRUGGLING IN THE REPRODUCTION

The school heads' responses pointed out that reproducing or printing the modules is the biggest challenge. Lack of resources forced school heads to solicit printing equipment and materials.

Accordingly, IDI01 expressed:

"Syempre sa atong supply nga printing equipment, sa printer palang naa natay shortage sa school then bigla kita ang nag print so dili kaya sa atong MOOE."

(At first, we had a problem with the shortage of printing equipment. Printers were insufficient to provide printouts that we need to produce and our school MOOE is not enough to cater all the needed modules for our learners.)

IDI02 explained:

"Kana lang siguro madugay, kanang delayed nila nga printing sa module kasi madelay man pud gud among process sa eskwelahan."

(The delay of printing and delivery of modules also caused the delay of distribution processes in our school.)

IDI04 narrated sensibly:

"Kasi ang school ang unang gumawa ng mga modules hindi kasi yung DepEd central office, ang school, naghahanap ng bond paper, naghahanap ng ink, naghahanap ng printer. So duon talaga ang pinakamahirap."

(It is the school who made modules first and not the central office. The school purchased and provided bond paper, ink, and printers to supply the needs for reproduction of modules for our learners. That is the hardest part.)

IDI08 relatively shared:

"As a school admin naeksperyens nako nga manguli namig alas 7 or alas 9 sa gabei because of the printing of modules. Because magstart na ang klase labi na kadtong naay dry run so kaylangan naming makaprint kay para maka dry run mi."

(As a school head, I experienced going home late because of the printing of modules; classes were about to start, especially those who have to undergo dry run, that is why we ought to print and reproduce.)

From the survey, limited resources are one of the reasons school heads struggle to reproduce self-learning modules.

Today, COVID-19 is still damaging the country, and among those who were drastically affected was the education sector. For instance, the reproduction of learning modules in time for the opening of classes urged administrators to find additional sources for reproducing and printing modules.

Some educators stressed that they encountered different problems like lack of printing equipment and materials in the market, delayed printing of the modules caused by the delay of delivery, and scarcity of printing materials. These challenged the school administration and hindered the delivery of modules to the learners.

In line with this, Olamo et al. (2019) supported this statement based on their research. However, the modular curriculum has not been successfully realized due to some challenges like the struggle to reproduce materials and lack of available resources supply of facilities and materials. Therefore, to ensure that the curriculum was effectively implemented, the essential materials, supplies, facilities, internet services, etc., should be made available to create favorable conditions for teachers, students, and administrators.

Also, Casilao (2020) supported that in modular distance learning, teachers were the ones who suffered the most because they were compelled to reproduce these modules despite tight resources. Further, school heads were also agonized by the inadequacy of printing materials and the expensive reproduction of self-learning modules that may hinder the delivery of learning to our students.

CHAPTER 11
GIVING SUPPLEMENTARY MATERIALS

The survey unveiled that supplementary materials are provided to learners to reinforce the modules. Also, this can be a good source of additional information that widens their learning. And this was what the participants observed to help improve students' reading and writing skills.

IDIo1 narrated with conviction:

"Every week maghatag mi ug reading materials. Kung lower grade maghatag sila ug 10 words, which is English mga CBC parttern. Sa Filipino mga 2 syllables tapos in higher grades mga reading comprehension nga story ang ipabasa. Eattach nila every magkuha ug modules."

(Every week, we provided reading materials to our learners, such as 10 CBC words in English. In Filipino, we provided 2 syllables for lower grades; for higher grades, stories for reading comprehension were also provided.)

Likewise, IDIo2 expressed:

"Ang among Initiatives and practices sa school sa modular scheme. Together with the teaching force nato sa skwelahan nagapadala mi ug kanang gitawag nato nga activity sheets,

supplementary activity sheets ang among mga bata.”

(One of the initiatives and practices in school in the modular system was giving our learners supplementary activity sheets.)

Relatedly, IDIo8 persuaded:

"Nagahatag jud mi ug mga supplementary learning materials nga maka support sa learning. Mga reading materials nagapadala jud mi sir, halimbawa mag distribute ang teacher ug kanang modules nagapadala jud mi ug reading materials.”

(We gave supplementary materials to support our students' learning; these reading and supplementary materials were distributed to their parents during the distribution of modules.)

Based on the participants' responses, giving supplementary materials helped improve students' reading and writing skills.

Instructional materials are vital in delivering instructions. The teacher's resources in teaching helped to achieve desired learning objectives. It ensured the students' solidifying learning experience to make learning more fun and exciting. Participants uttered that they gave instructional materials to the learners when parents got the modules in school. Moreover, they believed that providing individual copies of reading materials would help the students engage in reading activities and follow the flow of discussion for better understanding. That signified the positive effect of learning materials in the teaching-learning process.

In line with this, Melton (2014) confirmed that giving instructional materials can increase student achievement by supporting student learning. School heads reiterated in implementing the modular distance learning that they provided reading materials, Learning Activity Sheets (LAS) based on Most Essential Learning Competencies (MELC). These instructional materials were intended to improve the quality of education for the effective academic performance of students in schools.

In addition, Effiong and Igiri (2015) observed that having different instructional materials made learning natural and permanent. It was an essential and significant tool for teaching and learning to promote teachers' efficiency and improve students' performance. The instructional materials were also of great help, mainly that most self-learning modules were limited on explanation, definition, and activities.

CHAPTER 12
COPING MECHANISMS OF ELEMENTARY SCHOOL HEADS IN THE NEW NORMAL

The survey revealed the school heads applied varied strategies to cope with the challenges they encountered as elementary school heads on modular distance learning in the new normal and elicited themes from the transcriptions. Five (5) major themes emerged after I evaluated the responses of the participants, and these were the following: (1) being positive; (2) collaborating with the school community; (3) working to serve the learners; (4) establishing open communication system; and (5) seeking God's help

Table 2 presents the major themes and core ideas on how elementary school heads address the challenges of modular distance learning in the new normal.

Table 2. Coping Mechanisms of Elementary School Heads in the in the New Normal

Major Themes	Core Ideas
Being Positive	• Thinking positive for the good of the school • being positive to adopt the new normal • Taking the lead despite the problems and having a positive vibe • Being optimistic to face the situation • Thinking on the positive effect of the pandemic to stay stress-free in the new normal

Collaborating with the School-Community	• Asking opinions from the teachers, internal and external stakeholders • Consulting with teachers, PTA, and stakeholders before deciding • Involving the teachers and stakeholders from the planning to the implementation and monitoring • Leading the school in collaboration with the parents and community • Accepting help from graduates who volunteered in the reproduction of modules
Working to Serve the Learners	• Working because of the learners • Being motivated to continue the education of the learners • Thinking of the continuity of students' education despite the pandemic • Working for the benefit of the students and the country • Delivering education in these challenging times so that no one will be left behind
Establishing Open Communication System	• Calling parents directly and talking to them even in the absence of face-to-face • Giving cellphone numbers to parents for their inquiry • Having group chat with parents by grade level to clarify issues and concerns
Seeking God's Help	• Praying for God's help for the school head to cope with the problems • Praying for the future and this school year • Trusting in the Lord to easily cope with the challenges

Participants employed different strategies to cope with their challenges as elementary school heads in implementing modular distance learning in the new normal. With the challenges and struggles they experienced, they had found means and sources of encouragement to cope with and endure this endeavor.

There were five (5) significant themes that emerged out of the analysis of data, and these were the following mechanisms mentioned by the participants: (1) being positive; (2) collaborating with the school-community support; (3) working to serve the learners; (4) establishing open communication system; and (5) seeking God's help.

CHAPTER 13
BEING POSITIVE

Having a positive attitude was one of the coping mechanisms of the school heads as they experienced challenges and difficulties.

IDI03 revealed:

"Siguro as a school head we should have a balance nga mindset and always positive in those challenges nga ma encounter sa implementation nato sa Modular Distance Learning."

(As a school head, we should have a balanced mindset and always be positive in facing all the challenges we encountered during Modular Distance Learning implementation.)

In the same way, IDI06 opened up:

"So dapat ikaw talaga ang unang mag think positive that we can do it to look ways and means na maka adopt kayo sa new normal so yun sir."

(As School heads, we must be the first to think that we can do it positively and find ways and means to adapt to the new normal.)

IDI07 situated valiantly that:

"As a school leaders ikaw jud ang mag-una, ikaw jud ang mag take the lead and have positive vibe despite the problem naa lang gihapon naga look forward sa straight nga

dalan para sa kadaugan sa department of education."

(As School leaders, we must be the first to take the lead and have positive vibes despite this challenge, we are always here looking forward to the betterment of our department.)

Further, IDIo9 added:

"As school leaders, you should be optimistic enough to face the scenario with positivity, so you have to be surpassed and meet the needed thing that we have to do."

(As school leaders, we should be optimistic enough to face this situation to surpass and meet the needed things that we have to do.)

Eventually, IDIo10 quoted:

"Just think on the positive side of what is happing to cope with all the challenges we face, and I also impart teachers in planning. I always told them that this pandemic has brought something positive good to us."

(We must think on the positive side of today's scenario to cope with all the challenges we face. Impart our teachers in planning. I told them always that this pandemic brought something positive good to us.)

The responses mentioned above spoke of the coping mechanism of the school heads. Despite the problems faced by the participants, it is observable that they remained positive in their journey towards the implementation of modular distance learning. It helped them approach the ebbs and flows with the possibility that things would go well.

Being Positive

The participants' overall response pointed out that one way of coping with the challenges of modular distance learning was by being positive. Being optimistic kept a motivated and dynamic leader pursuing what s/he wanted with determination, ambition, and happiness. Being positive helped one focus on their vision and made every day a happy day. Further, being optimistic and overcoming negative thoughts could handle stress every day more constructive and improve one's quality of life.

Heathfield (2020) supported that having an optimistic outlook will positively impact one's health, happiness, and performance. Optimism is one factor that can affect success and self-fulfillment. Being positive is imperative to address problems in the new normal scenario. School heads must serve as beacons of hope to their co-teachers in these nasty changes in learning delivery. In addition, they must possess a positive attitude to make tasks light and easy to accomplish.

Moreover, this claim was also supported by Reh (2020), who stated that being a positive leader can boost and motivate their members to be more compassionate to realize the department's success. In this natural catastrophe that we experienced, many felt overwhelmed and even helpless, but having a more positive outlook can help school leaders, teachers, and stakeholders be more productive, efficient, and easily manage tasks.

CHAPTER 14
COLLABORATING WITH THE SCHOOL-COMMUNITY

School heads addressed the challenges smoothly because the community's support was always behind them. Working with the community nurtures the schools for their needs.

IDIo2 happily elucidated her experience; he said:

"Kinahanglan jud siya ug thorough planning para naay direction, Ing-ana nato siya pag deal. Also, asking opinions from others pud from my teachers and to the internal and external stakeholder's."

(There's a need for thorough planning to have a clear direction to deal with this situation, asking opinions from teachers and internal and external stakeholders could also help.)

Also, IDIo4 convincingly shared:

"As school head do not decide right away so think it 1000 times. Tama ba itong gagawin ko, and then you need to consult also your co-teachers. You need to meet with your PTA president and other stakeholders. Please advise me, anong gagawin natin."

(As a school head, I need to think a thousand times before making decisions and have to consult the teachers, PTA president, and other stakeholders to come up with a better decision.)

Similarly, IDI06 divulged even boldly:

"From the planning, implementation, and even addressing the challenges and issues. Stakeholders are involved, including teachers andyan talaga sila dapat, and I did not do it alone I have with me the stakeholders for the planning, implementation down to monitoring."

(From the planning, implementation, monitoring, and addressing the challenges and issues on Modular Distance Learning modality, teachers and stakeholders should always be involved for better decision-making.)

IDI07 shared her experience in overcoming difficult situations by saying,

"The best initiative in our school in the modular scheme is openness to the stakeholders, presentation of the programs, the projects through a virtual presentation, tanan nga mga stakeholders, tanan nga mga parents are invited to attend."

(The best initiative we had in our school in this Modular scheme was openness to stakeholders. The school's programs and projects were presented virtually, and everyone was invited to witness and listen.)

In the same way, IDI09 revealed:

"We have asked some volunteers to help us with the reproductions, especially yung bagong graduate they offer the spirit of volunteerism."

(We asked some volunteers to help us reproduce modules, especially those newly-graduated students who had the spirit of volunteerism.)

Thus, collaborating with the school community is imperative for implementing modular distance learning modalities.

Collaborating with the School-Community Support

Despite the challenges encountered in implementing modular distance learning, the participants expressed the importance of collaboration with the school community for the continuity of education in this COVID-19 pandemic. In any program Implementation, it is hard to stand alone. It is better to gain strength and reach success with lesser struggles. Having collaborative effort is already a trend since each party will have benefits if the program implemented is productive. Also, the additional strength and initiative of the internal and external stakeholders will motivate the implementers to fast-track their work for the materialization of success.

Saxena (2014) supported that stakeholders' engagement in school is imperative to development and success. A healthy relationship between leaders and other stakeholders is significant because this will allow everybody to work together, positively impacting the school harmoniously. For example, "It takes a village to raise a child." We can't rely on the department's budget to address the challenges in implementing modular distance learning. That's why we needed to work as a community to nurture our schools for our particular community needs.

Furthermore, Montemayor (2019) elucidated that Education Secretary Leonor Briones confirmed the importance of a strong partnership between the Department of Education (DepEd) and local government units (LGUs) in providing quality education. In the implementation of modular distance learning, the support of our stakeholders was essential; they helped us provide materials printing equipment and lent their vehicles to deliver the modules from the division office to the designated schools.

Chapter 15
Working to Serve the Learners

Ultimately, it gave the school heads a great feeling of self-satisfaction when they saw their students achieve in life and continued education despite this pandemic—working to serve learners was found to be one coping strategy of the participants.

IDI01 shared with conviction:

> *"Always para sa bata, why we chose education mao jud na akoa to serve our learners kay dili lang kay because we earned and received salary kay kumbaga I'm working because of those learners."*

> (We choose education for our children; we choose to serve not because of the salary but because of our learners.)

IDI02 positively shared how he deals with these challenges, he said:

> *"What motivates me the most? to continue the learning kasi, ma motivate jud ko nga unta ang mga bata dili maputol ilang pag tuon."*

> (What motivated me the most is the continuity of our children's learning, and I hoped their education would not stop.)

With confidence, IDI04 shared:

"For me ah sugakod jud first quarter lang nakita na nako ni kayang kaya, basta nasa puso molang na para sa bata, nga sayang pud mastop with in a one-year tungod lang sa pandemic."

(For me, it is challenging; in the first quarter, I already foresaw that we could do this as long as we think for the betterment of our learners.)

IDI05 positively shared how he dealt with these challenges, he said:

"To help our pupils, to transmit the learning. Because sino ang mag benefits is the learner, kasi yung learners, para sa bata yon yung tinatwag nila na para sa bata, para sa bayan."

(To help our pupils let's do everything to learn because they are its benefactors. Like they said, *"Para sa Bata, para sa Bayan".)*

With confidence, IDI06 shared:

"What motivates me? yung despite this challenges time, yung mga learners natin continue parin yung education and nobody well left behind and madeliver parin yung education to our learners despite this challenging time."

(What motivated me? It was seeing our learners continue their education despite this time of pandemic; let's face challenges to hold on and stand for their better future.)

Working to Serve the Learners

Generally, most participants believed that serving learners is essential for the school's harmonious governance.

Also, they stated that to care deeply about student success and recognize that test scores are not the only measure of quality education. By connecting themselves in all perspectives of the school system, school leaders monitored daily activities and emerging concerns. As a result, a visionary leader with practical communication skills and a desire to provide diverse students with an exceptional education may have what it takes to serve in the role of school heads confidently.

In addition, School heads should formulate a vision for effective teaching student achievement in learning, moral, cultural, mental, and physical development. It also prepares students for adult life to be well-mannered and well-educated citizens.

To support the learners,' The Department of Education (2019) disseminated *Sulong Edukalidad* as a response to the government's key priority of providing access to quality education which is an endeavor to address the gaps in basic education to ensure that no Filipino learner would be left behind. In this new normal education, teachers and school heads demanded upskilling and reskilling through a transformed professional development program and engagement of all stakeholders for support and collaboration.

In adherence to serving learners, Republic Act (11494) was promulgated last September 2020. Section 4 (n) of the *Bayanihan Act* mandated subsidies and allowances to qualified learners in private and public elementary and secondary education whose families were now facing financial crises due to loss of jobs and closure of enterprise community quarantine. This ratification's rationale was to help learners with financial assistance to continue learning despite this natural catastrophe.

Moreover, to support Filipino learners' education, health, and nutrition Republic Act (11310), known as The *Pantawid Pamilyang Pilipino Program* (4Ps), President Rodrigo signed last April 2019 Duterte. This served as a national poverty reduction plan of the government that gave conditional cash allowance to the poorest families. The 4Ps program was a big help to schools to eradicate poverty and teach how to become responsible parenthood. Every month, they conducted a Family Development Sessions DFS to teach parents about their parental roles and responsibilities, particularly children's health and nutrition, education, protection, and psychosocial needs.

Lastly, Abu (2020) asserted that every Filipino has the noble right to access quality education amid the crisis in our country. School heads in this new normal education had the most significant role in continuing the education of Filipino learners while assuring the health, safety, and welfare of all students, educators, and personnel of the education department.

CHAPTER 16
ESTABLISHING OPEN COMMUNICATION SYSTEM

Generally, most school heads believed that establishing an open communication system was essential for harmonious governance.

IDI01 revealed:

"Ako man gud I talk with the parent, ginakuha nako ang attention sa parent dili man mi mag face to face but sometimes I call the attention sa parent ako mismo directly motawag sa parent ana."

(I have talked to the parents, I got their attention through calling them since we couldn't give them face-to-face orientation.)

In the same way, IDI05 shared:

"We give the cellphone number to our parents for them to ask questions when there are activities, which is hard for them to answer or clarify. They can call our teachers so that we can extend our service to them."

(One of the practices was to give cellphone numbers to our parents so that they could easily contact the advisers for clarifications on the activities in the modules.)

Also, IDI07 valiantly shared how the communication system has lessened their burdens; he said:

> *"Naa jud mi mga individual group chat sa parents may mga communications nga pagahitaboon per grade level may mga representative to answer and to clarify sa mga issues nga moabot mga concerns sa mga parents."*

> (The advisers established class group chat so that the parents could easily access and communicate whenever they had difficulties with the lessons and activities in the modules.)

Therefore, effective communication will lead everyone to be on the same page, moving in the same direction toward the same goal.

The participants' overall response showed that one way of coping with the difficulties of modular distance learning (MDL) was by establishing open communication, even if the face-to-face transaction was not preferable due to the increased COVID-19 cases.

In this new normal education, school heads needed to create group chats on Facebook messenger. If teachers, parents, and learners had concerns about the Self-learning modules (SLM's), schools' management, school programs, school heads could quickly address them. It was also essential to have a smooth flow of implementation in schools. It allowed teachers' internal and external stakeholders to be more engaged and understand what mattered in the success.

Lastly, it will lead everyone to be on the same page, moving in the same direction toward the same goal.

Concerning this, Vdovin (2017) supported that establishing open communication in the organization resulted in that personnel being more likely to trust each other as a team where members love to work with each other and push each other to achieve improvement in the company. Establishing an open communication system in this pandemic was highly encouraged since we adapted the alternative working arrangement (AWA) in schools so we can easily call the attention and monitor the activities of the teachers.

Moreover, Hassell (2019) confirmed that establishing an open communication system in the department will lead to high-performing teams. It is a concept that almost all organizations are valued. Effective communication helped employees stay positive and productive. In implementing modular distance learning, having an open communication system will help students with queries or clarification about their modules. Teachers could follow up and monitor students' learning outcomes through these initiatives.

CHAPTER 17
SEEKING GOD'S HELP

Most School Heads stressed the importance of seeking God's help as coping mechanisms to address the challenges and issues of modular distance learning.

IDIo2 revealed that we need to faith in God, he said:

"Giunsa pag cope up, Smile lang jud sir? para sa akoa prayer, pag-ampo jud then smile spreading the smile kasi kitang tanan nagproblema. Palapdag share sa akong smile ug pag sabot."

(A simple smile is one of the coping mechanisms. For me, prayers are our greatest weapon. All of us encountered problems but smiling could ease our burdens.)

In the same way, IDIo3 shared:

"Whatever nga naay issues and challenges, chill lang. Ana ko sa mga teacher if ever naay mga challenges chill lang ta, wala jud tay laing mahimo epray nato atong mga dalan, let us pray for our futures let us pray this school year, let us pray for the children let us pray for everybody."

(In whatever issues and challenges that may come in this new normal, we need to relax and be calm. In this time of the pandemic, there's nothing we can do but pray. Let us pray for our future, for this school year, our safety, and the safety of our learners and everybody around us.)

Also, IDI07 valiantly shared how trust in the Lord have lessened their burdens, she said:

"Siguro gyod ang pinaka ano nako nganong dali nako na cope ang challenges, isa ang trust the Lord. Sa mga challenges mag offers jud sa "iyaha" kay ngano dili man ta perfect nga pagka lider."

(My weapon to manage and cope with these challenges is trust in our Lord, we need to surrender to Him everything like hardships and worries that this new normal has brought us.)

The following themes revealed the realities of school heads on the coping mechanisms of problems on modular distance learning in the new normal. Whether experienced or not, these issues were the basis to delve into deeper that it may be alleviated or be given remedy to these existing conditions.

Results revealed that most participants sought God's assistance when they could not handle a situation like the continuous onslaught of the COVID-19 viruses. Instead, they always prayed and asked for guidance to deliver quality education despite the situation.

According to (Bibleinfo.com), God promised to cover the entire range of our needs, troubles, and problems. He wanted us to hold on to these promises for help whenever we needed Him. These promises were as essential for Christian living as food and drink are for physical life. Even if one were an intellectual and prominent person, there were things that he/she can't control, and the only solution was to try to hold on and to seek God's providence.

In addition, Sharp (2019) confirmed that seeking help is vital for everyone and our society. It's a sign of strength and courage. It reduced the expense and impact of weakness and allowed more people to grow, flourish and contribute to a more positive community. Seeking help should be seen as a positive step in enhancing health, well-being, and happiness. Unfortunately, some circumstances were out of control, and things didn't go as planned. Instead, God calls us to trust Him to work for his glory and our good even in our darkest times.

CHAPTER 18

EXPERIENCES AND PRACTICES OF THE ELEMENTARY SCHOOL HEADS

After an in-depth analysis of the responses of the participants, four (4) major themes transpired, and these were: (1) school leaders should be versatile; (2) school monitoring and evaluation system should be intensified; (3) partnership with the stakeholders should be valued, and (4) lessons should be simplified.

Table 3 displays the major themes and core ideas on the insight drawn from the experiences and practices of the elementary school heads on the modular distance learning in the new normal.

Table 3. Experiences and Practices of the Elementary School Heads

Major Themes	Core Ideas
School Leaders Should Be Versatile	• Leaders should be creative in finding unique ways in implementing the MDL • School head should be flexible to face the challenges • Leaders should think outside the box to improve the implementation of MDL • School head should have diverse personality should be well rounded
School Monitoring and Evaluation	• Schools should have separate monitoring tools for the quality of learning

System Should Be Intensified	• School heads should have a monitoring and evaluation team • Every program and activity that the school implemented needed to be monitored and evaluated • Administrators should give time to assessing students' learning
Partnership with the Stakeholders Should Be Valued	• Leaders should work with partners to successfully implement modular distance learning • Leaders need to closely work with the stakeholders in planning and decision-making • Leaders should have a strong partnership because "no man is an island."
Lessons Should Be Simplified	• Mathematics lessons should focus on the (four) 4 basic fundamentals and not on complicated word problems • Lessons should be simplified without changing to suit to the level of the students • Modules should be concise and should limit the activities so as not to stress the students

After portraying best practices in implementing modular distance learning and encountering some challenges, the participants somehow gathered some realizations. These insights were helpful to other school heads and worth sharing for the significant improvement of school management.

After an in-depth analysis on the responses of the participants, four (4) major themes transpired, and these were: (1) school leaders should be versatile; (2) school monitoring and evaluation system should be intensified; (3) partnership with stakeholders should be valued, and (4) lessons should be simplified.

Chapter 19
School Leaders Should Be Versatile

Leadership versatility allows school leaders to solve problems, improve innovation, and achieve improvements in learning effectiveness and teacher engagement. Moreover, the participants expressed different insights on coping with the challenges and issues in implementing modular distance learning.

IDI01 revealed:

"I will also bring the implementation to our school that is why kailangan nato maging creative, maging naa tay mga best practices pag abot sa school."

(We need to be creative, execute best practices, and bring this to the school for implementation.)

In the same way, IDI03 opened up:

"Point of views as a school head you should have to kana ganing flexible siya, and always positive in those experiences' nga naay ma encounter nga challenges sa modular distance learning (MDL)."

(As school heads, we should be flexible and positive thinkers in dealing with the issues and challenges we face in modular distance learning (MDL.)

IDIo6 situated valiantly that:

"To be more creative and think outside the box ano yung mga possible ways na maaring maimplement natin for the improvement of MDL modality."

(Be creative in thinking of ways to implement better and improve Modular Distance Learning modality.)

Eventually, IDIo8 quoted:

"Kung school head ka, diverse pud ka dili lang ang learners ang diverse ang teachers pud in all aspect dapat naa kay kahibalo so kanang, well-rounded ka."

(As school heads and teachers, we should also be diverse and well-rounded persons like the way we think of our learners as diverse.)

Based on the participants' responses, being versatile and well-rounded leaders, they could develop their leadership styles to fit the present situation. Thus, they generated innovative ideas which can augment the implementation of MDL.

Another experience and practice of elementary school heads implementing modular distance learning in the new normal are proactive and versatile. Versatile leaders are resilient, and they can modify their leadership style according to how they want to influence or lead the school. It also gives a broad scope of teaching approaches and interaction with others. In these challenging times, school heads need to be well-rounded and think outside the box to influence others to develop programs and innovations that can augment the implementation of MDL to deliver quality education to our learners and improve learning effectiveness.

The work by Yukl and Mahsud (2010) confirmed that leaders should be versatile and adaptive in a world full of stress, difficulty, and changes. Leaders must possess a high commitment to do what is necessary and ethical. In this crisis, COVID 19 pandemic school heads must be versatile to overcome these challenges and create innovative ways to solve this predicament.

In addition, Schindler (2020) supported this claim in his work that versatility is an essential component of leading effectively in a dynamic, changing society. Versatile leaders have more interest in employees and persuasive teams. In this globalization era, it's necessary to cooperate with people with different backgrounds and ability levels effectively. In these challenging times, school heads must be well-rounded to approach the problems and find solutions.

CHAPTER 20
SCHOOL MONITORING AND EVALUATION SYSTEM

Intensified school monitoring and evaluation system were one of the participants' insights. School heads must continue to meet the divergent and changing demands of learners, teachers, and stakeholders.

IDI03 elucidated her experience, she said:

"I also had that monitoring tool separate from the division monitoring tool diba as you remember nag monitor ang region."

(I had school-based monitoring tools aside from the division and regional monitoring tools.)

Also, IDI05 convincingly shared:

"Kailangan, there should be a monitoring team sa school you have to create an evaluation team."

(School heads must create evaluation teams in their respective schools to implement Modular Distance learning.)

Similarly, IDI06 divulged even boldly:

"Another one the most important things during the monitoring and evaluation of MDL inadapt namin so in every program and activity that the school we implement kaakibat na diyan ang monitoring and evaluation."

(In every program and activity in school, it is very important to have monitoring and evaluation using the monitoring tools to supervise the implementation of Modular Distance Learning.)

In the same way, IDIo8 revealed:

"Mo assists si admin nga mohatag ug iyahang time to conduct ug assessment sa bata, sample kanang motawag sa parent to check and assess whether this particular student really knew about particular subject or lesson. Random checking sir murag ana ba."

(The school head can also make his own assessment through random checking to assess students' learning progress. He/she can call parents to check whether their children have learned what's in the modules.)

In overcoming the challenges of modular distance learning, correct information must be on hand to empower the school head to make the right and relevant decisions to facilitate appropriate managerial actions.

A school is where learning takes place, where formal education is taught to everybody that serves as a weapon in our daily life battles. School monitoring and evaluation are a fundamental part of the education system that will help improve programs and performance to achieve the result wanted.

Most participants stated that they had school-based monitoring and evaluation tools in implementing modular distance learning to cater to the learners' divergent and dynamic needs, teachers, and stakeholders. To address this, the data must be accurate to create the right and appropriate decisions and facilitate appropriate supervisory actions.

In line with this, Miller (2020) supported that schools' intensified monitoring and evaluation systems play an essential role in accountability and school improvement. School monitoring and evaluation system were only intensified if the collected data were correct and accurate. Through these, school programs and projects would improve, and the budget allocation would be allocated correctly.

Furthermore, to strengthen the monitoring and evaluation system, Paragoso and Barazon Jr (2019) confirmed that the Department of Education (DepEd) utilized the School Monitoring and Evaluation Assessment and Adjustment (SMEA) to improve the delivery of Basic Educational Services. Its main objective is to equip the school heads with essential data and insights on the status, progress, and results of education delivery. It's a tool to help school heads manage the schools efficiently and effectively and for the teachers to adhere to the teaching and learning process standards.

CHAPTER 21
PARTNERSHIP WITH THE STAKEHOLDERS

Stakeholders' evolvement is essential in ensuring the success of the program. This was the suggestion given by the participants to strengthen the implementation of modular distance learning.

IDI04 shared with conviction:

"So, in dealing that issues, challenges huwag mong sulohin as a school head you need to have a collaborative effort para mag success yong implementation ng Modular Distance Learning."

(The principal should not solve school problems and challenges independently; collaboration among teachers, PTA officers, and stakeholders is needed to implement Modular Distance Learning successfully.)

IDI06 positively shared how he dealt with these challenges; he said:

"As a leader hindi mo kailangan solohin lahat you have to involved specially in the planning down to the decision making."

(As a leader, one must consider the people in the school community and involve them in the decision-making for successful implementation.)

With confidence, IDI07 shared:

*"Kini lang gyod ang akoang ginahawakan is the
strong partnership kana bang no man is an
island, ayaw jud e ako-ako, nga kabalo jud ka
tanan, kanang naa sila sa palibot to help."*

(Building strong relationships with stakeholders
is my way to succeed in every implementation.
Don't be a one-man rule but seek the assistance
of people around.

Hence, valuing partnerships with stakeholders will establish good rapport interpersonal relationships that can help support the implementation of modular distance learning in the new normal.

In the Department of Education, stakeholders are generally known as individuals or groups' interests in the progress and success of an institution and its students. It included educators, faculty members, pupils, parents, and elected leaders such as Parents-Teachers Associations, municipality councilors, and state representatives. Participants clearly expressed that they valued the partnership of stakeholders because they had a greater capacity to produce positive change in schools, especially during the onslaught of covid 19 pandemics. In addition, stakeholders offered donations such as giving equipment to reproduce self-learning modules (SLM's). They also contributed to information dissemination regarding the modular scheme.

Inconsistency with valuing the partnership of stakeholders (DepEd Order No. 54, s. 2009) was released to give the value of the partnership of the stakeholders by establishing every elementary and secondary school Parents-Teachers Association (PTA). This group could help support the programs and projects in school and its essential companion, whose relationship is defined by being cooperative and open to dialogues to support the learners' benefit. The support of the (PTA) was a great help in modular distance learning in the financial aspect to augment this learning modality. They were also our partners in the retrieval and dissemination of self-learning modules.

In addition, valuing and recognizing the partnership of stakeholders in project management was essential to ensure the success of school projects. Most projects include multiple stakeholders, and each one can potentially speed up, slow down or completely obstruct the development. Stakeholders can also be highly beneficial to advocates, sponsors, and change agents (kahootz.com, 2020).

Moreover, Finkelstein and Repeta (2017) supported in their statements that a truly valued partner provided the opportunity to have candid and quality conversations to improve schools. To build effective education systems and productive learning settings, all stakeholders needed to come together significantly through valuing partnership and collaboration. In addition, they were significant assets in implementing modular distance learning by providing instructional materials and supporting programs implemented in school.

CHAPTER 22
SIMPLIFIED LESSONS

During the interview, simplifying the lessons in a modular scheme was one of the insights.

IDIo1 shared with conviction:

"Kung sa Mathematics four fundamentals sa addition, multiplication, division, and subtraction basic nalang sa jud ta unta wala lang ta ning-abot atong mga word problem nga pagka komplikado."

(In mathematics, there's no need to take up difficult word problems but only the four (4) fundamental, which are addition, multiplication, division, and subtraction. These were only the basics that students must learn.)

In the same way, IDIo4 shared his suggestion

for simplification of the lesson, he said:

"E simplify ang lesson pero dili nimo siya usabon you are going to simplify jud para masabtan into the lowest term of knowledge sa imong bata."

(Lessons in the module should be simplified according to the level of understanding and interest of our learners.)

IDIo7, with a deep breath, shared:

"Dapat e concise ang atoang mga modules kanang dili na gani siya super maka stress sa bata sample ha grade 1, 39 pages per subject in 1-week Dios ko, kanang we have to limit sa

(Lessons in the modules should be concise and stress-free for our learners; it should be limited to their level and understanding, especially those in Grade 1.).

Participants urged that lessons in self-learning modules must be simplified and focused on the tenets of good instruction and avoid ambiguities and complications.

Simplifying lessons following the level of the understanding and interest of our learners was essential to have effective and efficient learning outcomes. Participants' overall response revealed that in self-learning modules, lessons should be simplified and focused on the tenets of good instruction to avoid ambiguities and difficulties so that the learners could easily understand.

The study by Dangle and Sumaoang (2020) confirmed that in modular distance learning (MDL), the lessons should be simplified, reduce activities, and have more definitions for learners to understand easily. If possible, conduct a limited face-to-face to identify if students learned from the self-learning modules so that teachers could give immediate feedback and assistance.

In addition, Sundarasen et al. (2020) cited that students in the University of Malaysia were stressed by the overwhelming number of self-learning modules with unclear and confusing instructions, which hindered students' learning outcomes. In this new normal scenario, the challenges faced by learners had a significant bearing on their stress and anxiety levels. And as far as the student is concerned, the instruction and content of self-learning modules must be simplified, brief, and concise.

The above major themes were discussed, and cited literature was elaborated on the concept of modular distance learning modalities and the school heads' essential roles in implementing learning modalities. In these challenging times brought about by the COVID-19 pandemic, school heads, teachers, parents, and barangay council should work hand in hand to continue to deliver quality basic education. Maintaining good relationships with the stakeholders and school community is a significant factor in successfully implementing modular distance learning in the new normal. Further, modular distance learning can be more positively substantial if the department is strengthened by providing adequate and practical equipment for reproducing self-learning modules so that teachers have time to assist and monitor students' learning development.

NOTES

Chapter 1

Ancheta, R. F., & Ancheta, H. B. (2020). The New Normal Education: Challenge to the Private Basic Education Institutions in the Philippines. International Journal of Educational Management and Development Studies Volume 1, Issue 1.

Burns, J. (1978). Transformational Leadership Theory.

Burns, M. (2011). Distance Education for Teacher. Education Development Center, Inc.

Cheng, C. M., & Abu Bakar, M. B. (2017). The Impact of Using Modules in the Teaching and Learning of English in Malaysian Polytechnics: An Analysis of the Views and Perceptions of English Language Teaching,.

Dikshit , J., Santosh, P., & Garg , S. (2013). Pedagogic Effectiveness of Print, Interactive Multimedia, and Online Resources: A Case Bookof IGNOU. International Journal of Instruction.

Fayol, H. (1916). Henri Fayol's Principles of Management. Journal of Information Science Theory and Practice.

Hersey, P., & Blanchard, K. (1982). Situational Leadership Theory. Warner Books.

Manahan, J. (2020). DepEd says not all modules screened for quality; volunteer error spotters 'welcome'. Manila: ABS - CBN.

Vergara, A. M. (2017). Development, Effectiveness and Acceptability of Module for Problem Solving and Critical Thingking Skills of Alternative Learning System in District of Tanay II.

Chapter 2

Adonis , M. (2020). DepEd confirms 41 reported errors in modules. Philippine Daily Inquirer.

Bernardo, J. (2020). Modular learning most preferred by parents: DepEd.

Boholano , H., & Jamon, B. (2021). Teachers Lived Experiences In The New Normal In Philippine Public Schools: A Phenomenology.

Casilao, J. L. (2020). Teachers in remote areas struggle to deliver modules.

Dangle, Y., & Sumaoang , J. D. (2020). The Implementation of Modular Distance Learning in the Philippine Secondary Public Schools.

Dejene, W. (2019). The practice of modularized curriculum in higher. Cogent Education Volume 6.

Finol, M. (2020). Asynchronous vs. Synchronous Learning: A Quick Overview. Bryn Mawr College 101 North Merion Ave Bryn Mawr, PA 19010-2899.

Hernandez, R. (2012). Does continuous assessment in higher education support student learning? Higher Education, 64, 489–502.

Llego, M. (2020). DepEd Learning Delivery Modalities for School Year 2020-2021.

Nardo, M. B. (2017). Modular Instruction Enhances Learner Autonomy. American Journal of Educational Research, Vol. 5.

Olamo, T. G., Mengistu, Y. B., & Dory, Y. A. (2019). Challenges Hindering the Effective Implementation of the Harmonized Modular Curriculum: The Case of Three Public Universities in Ethiopia .

Sundarasen, S., Nurunnabi, M., Hossain, S., Sukayt , A., & Chinna, K. (2020). Psychological Impact of COVID-19 and Lockdown among University Students in Malaysia: Implications and Policy Recommendations.

Yoseph , T. G., & Mekwanent, T. D. (2015). The Suitability of te modular curriculum to offer / lean skill-based modules in EFL undergradutes classes.

Chapter 3

Aziz, N., Muda, M. S., Mansor, N. R., & Ibrahim, M. B. (2017). Literature review on instructional leadership practice among principals in managing changes. International journal of academic research in business and social sciences 2017.

Bautista, E. M. (2015). The Principal's Leadership Roles under R.A 9155.

Boogaard, K. (2020). 4 Times You Just Need to Suck it Up and Ask for Help at Work. Daily Muse Inc.

Buckner, K. (2020). The Role of Elementary and Secondary School Principals, Principal Duties and Responsibilities, Principal Qualifications.

Cuban, L. (2014). Teacher, principal, and superintendent core dilemmas that need to be managed.

Dangle, Y., & Sumaoang, J. D. (2020). The Implementation of Modular Distance Learning in the Philippine Secondary Public Schools.

Kelly, M. (2020). Qualities of a Good School Principal.

Krasnoff , B. (2015). Leadership Qualities of Effective Principals .

Leithwood , K., & Louis , K. (2011). Linking Leadership to Student Learning . Jossey-Bass; 1st edition .

Mahlangu , V. P. (2014). Strategies for Principal-Teacher Development: A South African Perspective. South Africa.

Meador, D. (2019). The Role of the Principal in Schools.

Muring, J. V. (2014). The Challenging Roles of School Principal.

Newell, J. M., Andreasen, K. J., & Medina, S. E. (2018). An Investigation of Professional Development to Prepare Secondary Administrators to Be Instructional Leaders in Technology Integration. Saint Louis University, ProQuest Dissertations Publishing.

Republic Act No. 9155. (n.d.). Governance of Basic Education Act of 2001.

Thakral, S. (2015). The historical context of modern concept of supervision.Journal of Emerging Trends in Educational Research and Policy Studies.

Chapter 4

Anderson, T. (2020). Area Principal Prepared for New Normal. OnFucos News.

Bender, L. (2020). Key Messages and Actions for COVID-19 Prevention and Control in School. Education in Emergencies, UNICEF New York .

Dangle, Y., & Sumaoang , J. D. (2020). The Implementation of Modular Distance Learning in the Philippine Secondary Public Schools

Department of Education. (2019). Sulong Edukalidad: DepEd's battlecry moving forward.

DepEd Order No. 15 s. 2020. (n.d.). Supplementary Guidelines on Managing Maintenance and Other Operating Expenses Allocation for Schools to Support the Implementation of Basic Education Learning Continuity Plan in Time of COVID-19 Pandemic.

Friday, H. (2020). Area Principals Prepared for New Normal. OnFocus.news.

Gunderson, G. (2020). Area Principals prepared for new normal. OnFocus News.

Hall , K. (2020). The New Normal: Five Insights from GOA's COVID-19 Leadership Roundtable.

Henebery, B. (2020). Coping with COVID: How principals are adapting to the new normal.

Jager , T. (2019). Best Strategies For Strengthening Relationships with Stakeholders.

Malipot, M. H. (2020). DepEd: Private schools allowed to open classes ahead of Oct. 5. Manila Bulletin.

McCarty, T. (2020). Area Principals Prepared for New Normal. OnFocus News.

Paragoso, S. D., & Barazon Jr, L. M. (2019). School Monitoring, Evaluation, and Adjustment (SMEA) in Central Cebu, Philippines.

Republic Act No. 11494. (2020). Bayanihan to Recover as One Act.

Rice, , M. F. (2020). Learning Continuity: Planning Considerations for School Leaders.

Teacher.org. (2020). What is Professional Development for Teachers?

Vergeire, M. (2020). DOH: School resumption in August safe if minimum health standards are observed. Manila Bulletin.

Watson, J. (2019). Blended Learning: The Convergence of Online and Face-to-Face Education. North American Council for Online Learning.

Chapter 5

Abu, E. (2020). Learning must continue in the new normal.

Ancheta, R. F., & Ancheta, H. B. (2020). The New Normal Education: Challenge to the Private Basic Education Institutions in the Philippines. International Journal of Educational Management and Development Studies Volume 1, Issue 1.

Briones, L. M. (2020). Learning Opportunities shall be available, The Basic Education Learning Continuity Plan in the Time of COVID-19. DepEd.

Coaching, C. H. (2019). How to Embrace Change and Become More You.

DepEd, Division Memorandum No. 188, s. 2020. (2020). Basic Education Learning Continuity Plan (LCP) Division of Bohol SY 2020-2021.

DepEd Order No. 54 s. 2009. (2009). Revised Guidelines Governing Parents-Teachers Associations (PTAs) at the School Level.

Effiong, O. E., & Igiri, C. E. (2015). Impact of Instructional Materials in Teaching and LEarning of Biology in Senior Secondary Schools in Yakurr Lg A.

Gura, I. (2019). 12 Reasons Why You Should Seek & Embrace Change.

Heathfield, S. (2020). Quotes About Optimism to Brighten Your Day.

kahootz.com. (2020). The importance of stakeholders in project management success.

Kouzes, J. M., & Posner, B. Z. (2012). The Leadership Challenge: How to Make Extraordinary Things Happen in Organization.

Madsen, S. (2020). Six principles for building trusting stakeholder relationships.

Melton, R. (2014). Objectives, competencies and learning outcomes. Developing instructional materials in open and distance learning.

Montemayor, M. (2019). DepEd-LGU partnership provides quality education: Briones.

Reh, J. F. (2020). Great Leaders Know How to Be Positive, Learn the value of a positive attitude.

Tingley, S. (2017). Principal Helpline: What are the 7 Habits of Successful Principals?

Saxena, A. (2014). Workforce Diversity: A Key to Improve Productivity.

Schindler, J. (2020). Versatile Leadership: How To Get Out Of A Workplace Rut.

Sharp , T. (2019). The Importance of Seeking Help .

Wallace Foundation. (2013). The school principal as leader: Guiding schools to better teaching and learning.

Yukl, G., & Mahsud, R. (2010). Why flexible and adaptive leadership is essential.

Chapter 6

Briones, L. M. (2020). Learning Opportunities shall be available, The Basic Education Learning Continuity Plan in the Time of COVID-19. DepEd.

DepEd, Division Memorandum No. 188, s. 2020. (2020). Basic Education Learning Continuity Plan (LCP) Division of Bohol SY 2020-2021.

Rice, , M. F. (2020). Learning Continuity: Planning Considerations for School Leaders.

Chapter 7

Jager , T. (2019). Best Strategies For Strengthening Relationships with Stakeholders

Madsen, S. (2020). Six principles for building trusting stakeholder relationships.

Chapter 8

Coaching, C. H. (2019). How to Embrace Change and Become More You.

Gura, I. (2019). 12 Reasons Why You Should Seek & Embrace Change.

Chapter 9

Adonis , M. (2020). DepEd confirms 41 reported errors in modules. Philippine Daily Inquirer.

Dangle, Y., & Sumaoang , J. D. (2020). The Implementation of Modular Distance Learning in the Philippine Secondary Public Schools.

DepEd Memorandum OUA MEMO 00-1020-0138. (2020). DepEd Error Watch Initiatives.

Chapter 10

Casilao, J. L. (2020). Teachers in remote areas struggle to deliver modules.

Olamo, T. G., Mengistu, Y. B., & Dory, Y. A. (2019). Challenges Hindering the Effective Implementation of the Harmonized Modular Curriculum: The Case of Three Public Universities in Ethiopia .

Chapter 11

Melton, R. (2014). Objectives, competencies and learning outcomes. Developing instructional materials in open and distance learning.

Melton, R. (2014). Objectives, competencies and learning outcomes. Developing instructional materials in open and distance learning.

Chapter 13

Heathfield, S. (2020). Quotes About Optimism to Brighten Your Day.

Reh, J. F. (2020). Great Leaders Know How to Be Positive, Learn the value of a positive attitude.

Chapter 14

Montemayor, M. (2019). DepEd-LGU partnership provides quality education: Briones.

Saxena, A. (2014). Workforce Diversity: A Key to Improve Productivity.

Chapter 15

Abu, E. (2020). Learning must continue in the new normal.

Department of Education. (2019). Sulong Edukalidad: DepEd's battlecry moving forward.

Republic Act 11310 . (2019). Act of institutionalizing the Pantawid Pamilyang Pilipino Program.

Republic Act No. 11494. (2020). Bayanihan to Recover as One Act.

Chapter 16

Hassell, D. (2019). Open Communication: Vital to Business Success.

Vdovin, A. (2017). The Benefits of Positive Communication in the Workplace.

Chapter 17

Bibleinfo.com. (n.d.). Have you ever cried out, "God help me!" Remember God knows all the troubles and problems that you face.

Sharp , T. (2019). The Importance of Seeking Help

Chapter 18

Schindler, J. (2020). Versatile Leadership: How To Get Out Of A Workplace Rut.

Yukl, G., & Mahsud, R. (2010). Why flexible and adaptive leadership is essential.

Chapter 19

Miller, D. (2020). Importance of School Monitoring And Evaluation Systems.

Paragoso, S. D., & Barazon Jr, L. M. (2019). School Monitoring, Evaluation, and Adjustment (SMEA) in Central Cebu, Philippines.

Chapter 20

DepEd Order No. 54 s. 2009. (2009). Revised Guidelines Governing Parents-Teachers Associations (PTAs) at the School Level.

Finkelstein, J., & Repeta, S. (2017). The Value of Partnership.

kahootz.com. (2020). The importance of stakeholders in project management success.

Chapter 21

Dangle, Y., & Sumaoang, J. D. (2020). The Implementation of Modular Distance Learning in the Philippine Secondary Public Schools.

Sundarasen, S., Nurunnabi, M., Hossain, S., Sukayt , A., & Chinna, K. (2020). Psychological Impact of COVID-19 and Lockdown among University Students in Malaysia: Implications and Policy Recommendations.

9 786218 307056